Doreatha Walker

Tyrah Ta'Sha Walker

Authors

THE DAY I MET AN ANGEL

(When Miracles Happen Right Before Your Eyes).

2
The Day I Met An Angel

Doreatha Walker and Tyrah Ta'Sha Walker

The Day I Met An Angel

(When Miracles Happen Right Before Your Eyes)

This book is for everyone who needs a miracle and those who do not think they are in need of a miracle.

The Day I Met an Angel
When Miracles Happen Right Before Your Eyes

Doreatha Walker

Tyrah Ta'Sha Walker

This book is for everyone who needs a miracle and those who do not think they are in need of a miracle.

God's Favor Is Real and His Miracles Are Miraculous

Divinity Empire Publishing Company

Houston, Texas

tryjesustoo@yahoo.com

Scripture quotations are taken from the King James Version of the Holy Bible.

The Day I Met An Angel

When Miracles Happen Right Before Your Eyes

Divinity Empire Publishing Company

6806 Lost Thicket Dr.

Houston, Texas 77085

ISBN: 978-1-61422-779-3

Printed in the United States of America

©2018 Doreatha Walker and Tyrah Ta'Sha Walker

No part of this book can be reproduced or transmitted in any form or by any means electronically or mechanically, including photocopying, recording, or by any information storage and/or retrieval system-without in writing from the publisher. Please send all inquiries to tryjesustoo@yahoo.com

Dedication

To everyone who believe in miracles and even if you do not, this book, is for you, for God's Glory.

This book is also dedicated to my magnificent husband, Terrance Walker, who has been my best friend, my love and has always been there for me.

This book is dedicated to Tyrah Ta'Sha Walker, our daughter, who has been the best child we could have asked

God for. Tyrah Ta'Sha Walker is also the co-author of this book.

This book is also dedicated to my mom, Alma Lee Long, who told me I can do anything and to always do my best.

This book is dedicated to my mother-n-law, Helen Wilson, who always believed in everything I was doing and told me to do it.

This book is also dedicated to my nephew who taught me that I could write my own book, because he wrote his and that with God, all things are possible and that the Worth of a Woman is priceless.

This book is dedicated to Naomi Long, my sister and best friend who always believe in me and always encouraged me daily.

This book is dedicated to my niece, Fredricka Williams who told me she wanted to be like me.

This book is dedicated to my big sister, Irene Franks Predom, who taught me how to read and do math, as well as how to do whatever I wanted to do in this life and my entire family for always lifting me up higher and believing in me.

Lastly, this book is dedicated to my little brother, Edward James Long, who meant the world to me. He supported me in everything I did. Rest easy, my little brother. He was simply the best brother I could have asked for.

CONTENTS

Dedication..............................7-10

Contents................................11-12

Acknowledgement.....................13

One......................................14-16

Two.....................................17-20

Three...................................21-24

Four....................................25-28

Five.....................................29-33

Six......................................34-37

Seven..................................38-47

References............................48-49

What Miracle(s) are you believing in? Write them......................50-53

Notes..................................54-57

About The Author, Doreatha Walker……………………………58-60

Pics of the authors…………………59

About the Co-author, Tyrah Ta'Sha Walker……………………………61

Pic of Co-Author………………62

Contact Information……………63

Back Page……………………………64

Acknowledgement

I want to acknowledge Jesus Christ for giving me the strength and the wherewithal to write this amazing book. Because of him, I breathe and have life. Thank you Jesus Christ for your Grace, Mercy and Favor.

Chapter One

In The Beginning

Jeremiah 33:3

Call unto me, and I will answer thee, and show thee great and mighty things. Which thou knowest not. (KJV)

It all began in January 1998 when I talked with my husband about having a child. We were excited for what God was getting ready to do in our lives. I went to the doctor to find out what all I needed to do to have a child. After looking at my files, the doctor said you will never be able to have a child and then he referred me to a specialist who said the same thing. This time, I did not remain quiet. I said to the doctor that I will be able to have a child because God blessed Abraham and Sarah and He will bless Terrance and I. The doctor looked at me as though he wanted to say, this foolish woman, but I believed the word of God and I just knew God would bless us with a child and that we would see a miracle happen, right before our eyes. See, I knew what God could do because I read it in God's word. You have to learn to believe the report of the Lord and not man. There will be so many times in our lives when we must believe God's word because He knows what is best for us. Many times, we believe the report of man and not the report of the Lord and we run into trouble, every time. Is it something you want to happen in your life? If it is, then go to the word of God and believe what it says, and you will be surprised when He makes the miracle happen right before your eyes. You must believe with all of your heart and soul, that God will never deny you of something He knows will be a blessing and beneficial for you and your family. Just believe and receive His blessings and His miracles.

"And when Abram was ninety years old and nine, the Lord appeared to Abram, and said unto him, I am the Almighty God; walk before me, and be thou perfect. I will make thee exceedingly fruitful, and I will make nations of thee, and kings shall come out of Thee. (KJV-Genesis 17, 1 and 6)."

Chapter Two

Jeremiah 29:11

I know the thoughts I think toward you, saith the Lord, thoughts of peace, and not of evil, to give you an expected end. (KJV)

While sitting in that hospital room after hearing the reports of the doctors, with my sister, Barbara, I knew that I had to begin calling on the Name of the Lord and that is exactly what I began to do. My sister asked me how I could be so calm when the doctor said I would never be able to have a child, and my reply to her was, when you believe the report of God and not the report of man, you could have a calmness and peace that no one can take. The doctor entered the room again. This time, he said, you would have to take the measles shot, because if you just happened to get pregnant, even after another doctor and I said you would never be able to have a child, your child would not have an immunity to measles. Now as he continued, I felt myself, calling on God more and more that day, knowing what this doctor was saying did not make any sense to me. Remember, he and another doctor told me that I would never be able to have a child, and now this same specialist, standing in front of me saying if I just accidentally get pregnant, our child would be blind, deaf, have special needs etcetera., and he continued to say, if you take this measles' shot, for sure you would not be able to get pregnant anyways for four months. This seemed to me like total confusion, and we know in Christ, there is no confusion. At that moment, I said to him again, God will bless Terrance and me with a baby. I do not believe the report of man, I believe the report of God. He looked at me and said, well then, do as you want. My sister and I gathered our things and walked out. I was heartbroken for a moment, but I knew God's word would not come back void and I believed God when His word stated to Abraham that he would make him father of many nations. I believed that principle for my husband, Terrance and me.

"And when Abram was ninety years old and nine, the Lord appeared to Abram, and said unto him, I am the Almighty God; walk before me, and be thou perfect. I

will make thee exceedingly fruitful, and I will make nations of thee, and kings shall come out of Thee. (KJV-Genesis 17, 1 and 6)."

So shall my word be that goeth forth out of my mouth: it shall not return unto me void, but it shall accomplish that which I please, and it shall prosper in the thing whereto I sent it. (KJV)

Chapter Three

Matthew 11, 28-29, (KJV)

Come unto me, all ye that labour and are heavy laden, and I will give you rest. Take my yoke upon you, and learn of me; for I am meek and lowly in heart: and ye shall find rest unto your souls. (KJV)

I remember driving home that day from the doctor's office and my heart was so hurt and I felt so disappointed. I realized something that day. I was looking through man's eyes, as I did every so often, instead of looking through the eyes of God. I knew when I look through the eyes of God, all hurt, disappointments, sadness and sorrow would be taken away. I cried, but I knew

God would work everything out. When I arrived home, I called my husband, Terrance, my sister, Naomi, my god-sister, Vanessa and my best friend, Jacqueline. I remember that day as though it was today. I was so overtaken with emotions, but I remember hearing from all of them, that God would work it out. Believe it or not, I knew He would, but I still was overcome with emotions. I decided that day, right then and there that I was going to pray Hebrews 11:1, each day.

Now faith is the substance of things hoped for, the evidence of things not seen. (KJV).

Throughout that day, I went on about my business and then a letter arrived in the mail, stating I needed to get an ultrasound on my breast, because they believed they had found something. Well, I had already had to call on God prior and that is exactly what I did again. I cried, but I knew already that I was going to pray Hebrews 11:1, believing that God would bless us with a baby, so I turned that over to God as well. The ultra sound came back negative, but can you imagine getting terrible news all in the same day? Can you imagine how some people would just throw in the towel? Well, I refused to do so. It is so amazing because I am tearing up right now, writing Tyrah Ta'Sha Walker's story. I knew God would do the supernatural in our lives. I believe the report of the Lord and I began praying Hebrews 11:1 everyday faithfully.

Now faith is the substance of things hoped for, the evidence of things not seen. Hebrews 11:1, (KJV)

Chapter Four
In the middle of it all

Psalm 37:4-5

Delight thy self also in the Lord; and he shall give thee the desires of thine heart: Commit thy way unto the Lord; trust also in him; and he shall bring it to pass. (KJV)

I remember as though it was today, when I was just doing different things around the house. I remember I was ironing, believing God would bless us with a child, so I had a pregnancy test at home. I decided to use it at that moment, and I could not believe my eyes. You have to move when God says move. I remembered thinking oh my God, our miracle has happened, but in my disbelief, looking through man's eyes, I said to myself, this is impossible because of what the doctors had said prior, even though, I had been praying for a miracle. I still could not believe it, so I decided to go purchase several pregnancy test and each one was positive. I cried so much, but this time it was because of the Joy God had given to us. I am tearing up right now. You have to understand the significance of God wanting to bless you. It is all because He and only He gets the glory. No one can never tell me what God cannot do. His miracles are real and they happen every day. We just have to see through the eyes of God, and we will see each and every miracle, regardless if they are large or small. Can you imagine the joy I had in my heart and spirit? Can you imagine how much excitement I felt and how grateful and thankful I was to God? See, when you pray for a miracle to happen, you have to make sure you let God know that it is not your will, but His will and your miracle will manifest itself.

God's word says, Jesus said to him," If you can believe, all things are possible to him who believes." Immediately, the father of the child cried out and said with tears, "lord, I believe; help my unbelief!" Mark 9, 23-24, (KJV).

See, I did not mention earlier, that I told God however you decide to work this situation out, we are well satisfied and that we know He has our best interest at heart. When I told God however He works it out, we are satisfied, and He heard me because it went from my mouth to God's ears. Do you know that at that moment, I surrendered everything to God?

I began totally looking through the eyes of God. I wanted Him to know that I gave my life to Him and my thoughts. I wanted Him to see that I was thankful and grateful no matter what. I wanted Him to know that I put my faith and trust in Him totally.

If you can believe, all things are possible to him who believes." Immediately, the father of the child cried out and said with tears, "lord, I believe; help my unbelief!" Mark 9, 23-24, (KJV).

Chapter Five

Jeremiah 33:3

Call unto me, and I will answer thee, and show thee great and mighty things, which thou knowest not. (KJV)

I could not wait to tell my husband, sister, god-sister and best friend, what the Lord had done. You would not believe what I did. I called all of them on the phone together, except my best friend, Jacqueline. I told them all together, my husband, Terrance Walker, my sister, Naomi Long and my God-sister, Vanessa Dightman Brown, and we made so much noise, it made my ears and head hurt. It was the best noise I had ever heard. We cried, we praised God and we were so very happy. I went to my husband's job with all of the pregnancy test in an envelope and I wish I had recorded the expression on his face. It was pure joy. What God has for you, is surely for you and no man can take it or tell you it is not yours. You have to believe it and receive it, name it and proclaim it in Jesus Sweet and Holy name, and it will be yours. Do you need to be healed? Do you need your financial situation taken care of? Were you told you will never conceive? Are you in heavy credit card debt? Are you about to lose your house, car and your mind? Well, give it to God, find a scripture in His word and meditate on it day and night and watch the miraculous miracle God will perform, right before your eyes. Now, remember, you have to surrender all to God and leave it in His hands by letting Him know, not your will but His will be done. I am praising God and shouting glory hallelujah for you right now, because I know He is getting ready to perform a miracle right before your eyes. I hope and pray you are giving Him all honor, glory and praise, believing like me, it is finished.

My husband, Terrance was so excited, my sister, Naomi and my God-sister, Vanessa were as well. The journey was just beginning for us. I went to the doctor and they confirmed that I was pregnant and stated that I was a high risk pregnancy and that I had to stop running up the stairs at home, exercising and my doctor later on did what is called a McDonald Cerclage, which was a cervical cerclage, where the doctor stitches your cervix shut, to keep the baby in. I knew God had given us our baby not to take back, so I was not worried at all. God was so amazing to us. He made sure everything went as plan. I had to go to the doctor every week, then it went to two weeks, then four weeks and then once a month. Do you know, God can do anything? Everything was awesome and God was always faithful to us.

Jeremiah 32:27, Behold, I am the Lord, the God of all flesh: is there anything too hard for me? (KJV)

Nehemiah 8:10

Then he said unto them, Go your way, eat the fat, and drink the sweet, and send portions unto them for whom nothing is prepared: for this day is holy unto our Lord: neither be ye sorry, for the joy of the Lord is your strength. (KJV)

Chapter Six

Jeremiah 29:11

For I know the thoughts that I think toward you; saith the Lord, thoughts of peace, and not of evil, to give you an expected end.

It came time to know the sex of the baby. We always said we would wait, but it was so suspenseful waiting, we decided to go ahead and see what the sex was. To our amazement, the doctor said we think it is a girl, but because of the fibroids, we could not see the baby's features at all. The ultrasound features of the baby actually looked like a snowman. Then she said, we think it is a boy, but she was unsure. In all actuality, she had no clue and we did not either. Really, it worked out exactly as it should have because we said in the beginning that we did not want to know the sex of the baby. My husband decided to paint the room blue. I remember telling him, you may not want to paint the room blue because the doctor is unsure concerning the sex of the baby, but he did it anyway.

I had to continue to go to all appointments and I remember it came the day when we had to make the decision if we wanted the amniocentesis and we said no. We believed that God did not bless us with the baby to think anything may be wrong, so we signed the proper paperwork, stating we did not want that test done. We never worried at all because God had been so good to us. We knew God was going to bless us with a healthy baby when that time came. See, it does not matter what miracle you are asking God for. You have to ask and believe that you will receive it, name and proclaim your miracle. You have to see through the eyes of God and not through the eyes of man. You have to surrender all to God and let him know that it is His will and not your will. You will be amazed at what God will do for you. Just like He blessed us, I know He will bless you too. Just believe and receive.

Luke 22:42, Saying, Father, if thou be willing, remove this cup from me: nevertheless not my will, but thine will, be done. (KJV)

Thessalonians 5:16, Rejoice evermore. Pray without ceasing. In everything give thanks:

for this is the will of God in Christ Jesus concerning you. (KJV)

Chapter Seven

The Rest of the Story

John 14:13-14,

And whatsoever ye shall ask in my name, that will I do, that the Father may be glorified in the Son. If ye shall ask anything in my name, I will do it. (KJV)

After several more visits to the doctor, it was delivery time. We were so excited, overjoyed, filled with amazement, gratefulness, thankfulness and the Holy Spirit. Do you know, God will take your disappointments, sadness, unbelief, worry, hurt and unfaithfulness away? Then later, replace it with so much love, joy, peace, gratitude, contentment, thankfulness and faithfulness? That is exactly what He did for us, when we began to look through the eyes of God and not the eyes of man. Every opportunity we had, we praised God for His amazing blessing.

Contractions came and we were so prepared. Bags packed, watch on Terrance's wrist to time the contractions and car ready. Can you imagine how our hearts were pounding with excitement and joy? We arrived to the Woman Hospital of Texas, but I had not dilated enough, so they sent us home. Do you know we went back that same day and they once again said, I was not dilated enough and I said the baby is about to come, so they put us in a room. The doctor, my angel, Dr. Theresa Robinson, had to induce labor because God had Tyrah

Ta'Sha Walker, who we did not know at the time was a girl, so secure in the womb, she did not want to come out. Do not tell me what God cannot do, because He can do all things. He can do the impossible. We just have to believe. I was in labor for 12 hours, but it did not matter because we were just so overjoyed. I remember I had back labor and my sister, Naomi Long and my husband Terrance Walker, had to put cold and hot packs on my back. After dilating 6 centimeters, I requested medicine and they gave it to me, but it did not help because, right after getting the medicine, the baby head crowned. I was told at the time, because I could not see our baby, that our baby had the most beautiful black hair. To our amazement, we were told we had a baby girl. I remember she was not crying because they were working on her because she had drank the amniotic fluid, which is very dangerous for a baby to drink. Then all of a sudden, we heard the most beautiful, loud cry I have ever heard, and it felt so good. I saw her dad, get her little finger and she immediately stopped crying. She knew his voice because he would talk to her every day. She knew his touch because he would always rub my stomach. What a joyous day. Tyrah Ta'Sha Walker was born at 4:30 that morning on March 17, 1999 and she was so precious and the best gift God could have ever given to us. The day I Met An Angel. We had to stay in the hospital extra days because her body temperature was low, but look at God, her temperature regulated and we were able to take our beautiful baby girl home.

Terrance was an awesome dad and he still is today. He spoiled his princess and he took excellent care of us. God is so good.

She has always been the best child ever. I nursed her for 14 months and her dad was there every step of the way. Terrance would change her and bring her to me to nurse. We were an amazing team, as we are now. I caught a bad cold and I had to take antibiotics that could harm her and that's the only reason I stopped nursing her.

We will never, ever forget what God did for us. He gave us a miracle right before our eyes and we will be forever grateful and thankful. The day I met an angel, Tyrah

Ta'Sha Walker. Tyrah was and still is the best child we could have ever asked God to give us. She did not cry much at all. She learned to work the computer at 2 years old, she spoke really well and she learned to read at 3 years old, where she had an unbelievable understanding of what she read and what was read to her. At three years old, Tyrah gave her life to the Lord. We enrolled her in school for a few days of kindergarten, but they did not want me to eat with her, so we took her out. I know that is so funny, but actually, it was one of the best decisions of her life. Afterwards, we decided to Home-school her until first grade. She has always excelled in school. God is so good. She took the SAT test in middle school and scored really high on it, she went to an Early College High School where she was able to take college classes in the 10th grade. She graduated from Community College with an Associate of Science before High School, received a huge scholarship at a prestigious university and she is majoring in Criminal Justice and plan to go to law school after her two years at the university. God has been so good to us.

Lastly, she plans on taking a year off to go to Cosmetology school, after she completes her Bachelor's degree and then go to law school. She is simply the best daughter we could ever have. She truly rocks. Now, I know you understand the magnitude and significance of why I wanted to write this story, because it truly was The Day I Met An Angel.

Romans 2:11, For there is no respect of persons with God.

We hope that this book will help you to receive and believe in your miracle because as God's word says, He has no respect of person and what He did for us, He surely will do for you. May God bless you and your family with miracles and remember, every day He performs miracles, big and small. We just have to look through the eyes of God to see them. Today, you may need to be healed from cancer, high blood pressure, diabetes, need to conceive. Whatever miracle you need, ask and it shall be done, believing that God does work miracles, regardless if they are big or small miracles, they are miracles.

Proverbs 3:5-6, Trust in the Lord with all thine heart; and lean not unto thine own understanding. In all thine way acknowledge him, and he shall direct thy paths.

Philippians 4:4-8, Rejoice in the Lord always: and again I say rejoice. Let your moderation be known unto all men, The Lord is at hand. Be careful for nothing; but in everything by prayer and supplication with thanksgiving let your requests be made known unto God. And the peace of God, which passeth all understanding, shall keep your hearts and minds through Christ Jesus. Finally, brethren, whatsoever things are true, whatsoever things are honest, whatsoever things are just, whatsoever things are pure, whatsoever things are lovely, whatsoever things are of good

report, if there be any virtue, and if there be any praise, think on these things.

References

Chapter One

Jeremiah 33:3

Genesis 17, 1 and 6

Chapter Two

Jeremiah 29:11

Genesis 17, 1 and 6

Chapter Three

Matthew 11, 28-29, (KJV)

Hebrews 11:1,

Chapter Four

Psalm 37:4-5

Mark 9, 23-24

Chapter Five

Jeremiah 32:27

Jeremiah 33:3

Nehemiah 8:10

Chapter Six

Jeremiah 29:11

Luke 22:42

Thessalonians 5:16

Chapter Seven

John 14:13-14

Romans 2:11

Proverbs 3:5-6

Philippians 4:4-8

What miracles are you asking God for?

Write them on the blank pages included in this book.

Miracles I am asking God for Right Now

Miracles I am asking God for Right Now

Miracles I am asking God for Right Now

NOTES

NOTES

NOTES

NOTES

About the Authors

Doreatha Walker loves the Lord and credits Him for everything and everyone in her life. She is married to Terrance Walker, her amazing husband who gives her the opportunity to work on different projects like this book and love her so much and support her endeavors. Doreatha has a Bachelor's of Science in Early Childhood Education and a Master's Degree in Educational Mid-Management from Texas Southern University, where she played basketball and hold many records, as well as named to an All American Team, while playing basketball. Doreatha was an Outstanding College Student of America recipient and on the Dean's List while there at Texas Southern University. Doreatha Walker was named a Who's Who recipient as well. Doreatha has a Master's Degree of Business Administration in Healthcare Management from the University of Texas at Tyler and credits everything to Christ. She has taught for 15 years and is also certified as a principal. Doreatha attends Greater St. Matthew Church, where her Pastor is Dr. Gusta Booker and Co-Pastor Rev. Ronald Booker. Terrance and Doreatha Walker has one daughter named Tyrah Ta'Sha Walker, who is the co-author and whom this book is written about. Doreatha Walker is a proud Alpha Kappa Alpha woman and she has a 501©3 organization, Heavens' WAY, where she transforms the lives of homeless and needy men, women and children.

Tyrah Ta'Sha Walker loves the Lord and credits God for all her achievements in life. She loves to dance and played the violin for many years. She graduated with honors from High School, where she earned an Associate Degree in Science from a Community College, while attending High School, and she is attending a prestigious university at this time. She majors in Criminal Justice, plans to go to Cosmetology school and then Law school. She is doing so many amazing things and plan on becoming a child advocacy attorney.

The Day I Met An Angel

Contact Information

Doreatha Walker, M.Ed. MBA, Author

Tyrah Ta'Sha Walker, Associate of Science, Co-Author

Divinity Empire Publishing Company

6806 Lost Thicket Dr.

Houston, Texas 77085

832 530-6674

Email tryjesustoo@yahoo.com

Watch God Perform A Miracle(s) Right Before Your Eyes

Scripture quotations are taken from the King James Version of the Holy Bible.

Divinity Empire Publishing Company

6806 Lost Thicket Dr.

Houston, Texas 77085

ISBN: 978-1-61422-779-3

tryjesustoo@yahoo.com

Doreatha Walker Author and Publisher

Tyrah Ta'Sha Walker, Co-Author

Printed in the United States of America

©2018 Doreatha Walker and Tyrah Ta'Sha Walker

www.ingramcontent.com/pod-product-compliance
Lightning Source LLC
Chambersburg PA
CBHW051709090426
42736CB00013B/2621